MW01002835

Talit ha Cumi

JOHN FRANCIS

CREATION
HOUSE
A STRANG COMPANY

TALIT HA CUMI by John Francis
Published by Creation House
A Strang Company
600 Rinehart Road
Lake Mary, Florida 32746
www.creationhouse.com

Unless otherwise noted, all Scripture quotations are from the are from the King James Version of the Bible.

Scripture quotations marked TLB are from The Living Bible. Copyright © 1971. Used by permission of Tyndale House Publishers, Inc., Wheaton, IL 60189. All rights reserved.

Cover design by Jerry Pomales

Library of Congress Control Number: 2007936688
International Standard Book Number: 978-1-59979-265-1

08 09 10 11 — 987654
Printed in the United States of America

This book is dedicated to:

- » My wife, Penny, whose depth and wealth of knowledge never ceases to amaze me

- » Prophetess Juanita Bynum, who gave me my first tallit

- » Rabbi James, for valuable insight into the Jewish religion and practices

Contents

A Personal Note

IT WOULD BE wrong of me to begin this book
without first mentioning briefly where my initial
interest in prayer was created. I grew up in a Christian
home where regular prayer was a normal part of my
daily life and routine. My father, the late Bishop T. G.
Francis, instilled in me the importance of a regular
prayer life. As a young boy, I never fully understood
or welcomed the 6 a.m. prayer sessions that we as a
family were expected to attend in our living room
each morning. There were no exceptions to this rule,
and I would have happily swapped an hour or two
on my knees for my warm bed and pillow any day!
Now that I am older, I am glad that my father took
the time to introduce me to prayer at such a young
age. I can honestly say that there have been so many
occasions in my life when I have been so grateful to
have the foundation of prayer to rely on in my Christian walk.

There truly is power in prayer, and as each season
of my life passes I find that I rely on prayer as an

integral part of my life more and more. I know that if it were not for prayer I wouldn't be alive today. My mother was diagnosed with cancer before I was born. My parents had been told by the doctors that my mother had a brain tumor which was inoperable and that she didn't have much longer to live. They had concluded that there was nothing they could do for her and had actually sent her home to die. The only help the doctors were able to provide was some pain relief medication. My father wasn't prepared to accept this fate for her and continued to pray for her healing. If the doctors couldn't do anything then he was sure that His God could! He didn't believe it was God's will that my mother should die. After much prayer and my father's obedience to God's Word, my mother was healed of cancer. I was born after my mother was healed, although the doctors advised my father that having more children could result in her death. My father believed that if God had allowed my mother to become pregnant then He would keep her through the pregnancy. My mother, Elfreda Francis, defying the odds not only gave birth to my sister, but became pregnant again and gave birth to me. My mother is still alive today—a living testimony to the power of prayer. I have seen the lives of many changed in remarkable ways because prayer was seen as a real and tangible solution to their impossible situations.

I remember speaking at the Praise Power Conference a couple of years ago on the subject of *Talit ha Cumi*. As I was preaching I felt led of the Lord to place the tallit I was using during the service on a lady in the congregation who was confined to a wheelchair. She immediately got up out of the wheelchair and started worshiping. I later found out that she had been completed healed of cancer that evening, and when I visited the same conference a year later she was still rejoicing, still completely healed, and she no longer needed the wheelchair.

Prayer is powerful and wonderful, and my desire is that all will discover the joy, strength, and peace that a dedicated life of prayer can bring.

Preface

*M*Y JOURNEY BEGINS with the growing popularity within the Christian community of a large piece of tapestry cloth measuring approximately six feet in length by four feet. I became intrigued by this sacred garment that has its roots in the Jewish community. As time passed I was becoming more curious about this piece of cloth and its association with prayer.

To be honest, when I was given my first prayer shawl, I wasn't really sure what I should do with it. I wanted to use the prayer shawl in the right way and at the right time. I had so many questions: Why was this beautifully embroidered piece of tapestry so closely linked with prayer? What, if any, was its significance or link with the Bible? Is it still relevant today? How should it be used? When should it be used? Was I, being non-Jewish—a Gentile—allowed to use it?

Its significant link to the Word of God and to prayer became real to me in a new way after hearing my wife,

Penny, teach and preach during our prophetic, prayer, and praise conference on the prayer shawl or, as it is properly termed, the *tallit*.

After hearing my wife's teaching I realized how strategic certain scriptures were. Although they seemed unrelated, they were in fact divinely linked by God. My questions were answered; it was amazing! Our family had lived in a Jewish community for several years, and I was now seeing my neighbors with new, enlightened eyes. Through a piece of cloth, God had revealed an ancient truth that revolutionized my prayer life.

The teaching in this book has changed my life and that of thousands. I hope and pray that it will do the same for you.

—BISHOP JOHN FRANCIS

Chapter 1

What Is a Tallit?

And the LORD spake unto Moses, saying, Speak unto the children of Israel, and bid them that they make them fringes in the borders of their garments throughout their generations, and that they put upon the fringe of the borders a ribband of blue: And it shall be unto you for a fringe, that ye may look upon it, and remember all the commandments of the LORD, and do them; and that ye seek not after your own heart and your own eyes, after which ye use to go a whoring: That ye may remember, and do all my commandments, and be holy unto your God.

—NUMBERS 15:37–40

Thou shalt make thee fringes upon the four quarters of thy vesture, wherewith thou coverest thyself.

—DEUTERONOMY 22:12

Would you be surprised to learn that the death of one man prompted the almighty God, *YHVH* (יהוה), to bring into effect a commandment that would affect millions of lives for thousands of years? Would you be amazed to know that God loves His people so much that He considered losing one man to sin, one too many? If someone told you that God had designed something to help His people to never sin again so that He wouldn't have to punish them, wouldn't you want to know what it was? If your answer is yes, then read on, because a spiritual revelation unfolds in the pages of this book that will radically change your life.

We begin with the story of a Hebrew man who went out on the Sabbath day to gather some sticks. We presume he needed the sticks to make a fire. At the time he was gathering the sticks he never imagined that this simple act would cost him his life. It wasn't the fact that he was gathering the sticks that was the problem. The problem was his timing. God had given commandments to His people that they had promised to adhere to. According to the Torah (Jewish book of the Law) God gave 613 commandments to His people.[1] Most people tend to concentrate on only ten of these commandments:

And the LORD said unto Moses, Write thou
these words: for after the tenor of these words
I have made a covenant with thee and with Israel.
And he was there with the LORD forty days and
forty nights; he did neither eat bread, nor drink
water. And he wrote upon the tables the words of
the covenant, the ten commandments.

—Exodus 34:27–28

And he declared unto you his covenant, which
he commanded you to perform, even ten
commandments; and he wrote them upon two
tables of stone. And the LORD commanded me
at that time to teach you statutes and judgments,
that ye might do them in the land whither ye
go over to possess it.

—Deuteronomy 4:13–14

You may worship no other god than me.
You shall not make yourselves any idols: no
  images of animals, birds, or fish.
You shall not use the name of Jehovah your
  God irreverently, nor use it to swear to a
  falsehood…
Remember to observe the Sabbath as a holy
  day…
Honor your father and mother…
You must not murder.
You must not commit adultery.
You must not steal.

You must not lie.

You must not be envious of your neighbor's house, or want to sleep with his wife, or want to own his slaves, oxen, donkeys, or anything else he has.

—Exodus 20:3–4, 7–8, 12–17, TLB

When God gave His commandments to Moses He made it clear that He had entered into covenant with Israel and that His people were to learn these laws and follow them. On the day that this man went to gather sticks he broke one of God's commandments. God had given a commandment to His people that they were to do no work on *Shabbat* (the Sabbath) and that they were to remember the Shabbat and keep it holy for Him. People tend to become caught up with one particular day of the week, but careful study has shown that in the Bible Shabbat is represented by a certain day of the week and times and seasons in the year. The word *Shabbat* (שבת) simply means "rest" or "repose"—a time to set aside for God and His service. God's people were instructed to remember His feasts and holy days and keep them sacred.

Behold, I build an house to the name of the LORD my God, to dedicate it to him, and to burn before him sweet incense, and for the continual shewbread, and for the burnt offerings morning and evening, on the sabbaths, and on the new moons, and on the solemn feasts of the LORD our God. This is an ordinance for ever to Israel.

—2 Chronicles 2:4

God had entered into a covenant (a relationship with promise) with His people. God had promised to bless them and their children and their children's children. He had promised to provide for them, make them rich and prosperous, and protect them as long as they were obedient to His commandments or laws.

> If you fully obey all of these commandments of the Lord your God, the laws I am declaring to you today, God will transform you into the greatest nation in the world. These are the blessings that will come upon you: Blessings in the city, Blessings in the field; Many children, Ample crops, Large flocks and herds; Blessings of fruit and bread; Blessings when you come in, Blessings when you go out. The Lord will defeat your enemies before you; they will march out together against you but scatter before you in seven directions! The Lord will bless you with good crops and healthy cattle, and prosper everything you do when you arrive in the land the Lord your God is giving you. He will change you into a holy people dedicated to himself; this

he has promised to do if you will only obey him and walk in his ways. All the nations in the world shall see that you belong to the Lord, and they will stand in awe. The Lord will give you an abundance of good things in the land, just as he promised: many children, many cattle, and abundant crops. He will open to you his wonderful treasury of rain in the heavens, to give you fine crops every season. He will bless everything you do; and you shall lend to many nations, but shall not borrow from them. If you will only listen and obey the commandments of the Lord your God that I am giving you today, he will make you the head and not the tail, and you shall always have the upper hand. But each of these blessings depends on your not turning aside in any way from the laws I have given you; and you must never worship other gods.

—Deuteronomy 28:1–14, TLB

It was really simple: they would receive every benefit they could ever think of as long as they were a holy people faithful to God. But this poor man broke a commandment about the Sabbath (*Shabbat*); he had sinned. It could have been any one of the commandments, but on this occasion he broke the one regarding *Shabbat*. It is clear from the text that the people didn't know what to do with him. The consequences of his sin were severe—death by stoning.

And they that found him gathering sticks brought him unto Moses and Aaron, and unto all the congregation. And they put him in ward, because it was not declared what should be done to him. And the LORD said unto Moses, The man shall be surely put to death: all the congregation shall stone him with stones without the camp. And all the congregation brought him without the camp, and stoned him with stones, and he died; as the LORD commanded Moses.
—Numbers 15:33–36

One man's death was enough. God immediately gave Moses instructions about their garments (Numbers 15:37–38). One man's fatal mistake moved God quickly into action. He told Moses to tell the people to put fringes on the hems or borders of their garments, and in the fringes they should put the color blue. God explained that He wanted His people to do this so they could look at the fringes with blue and remember the commandments that God had given them and keep them. He wanted His people to remember His laws and obey them. God didn't want anyone else to die. Every time they wore their garments, which roughly resembled cloaks, they would see the fringes with blue and remember. Every time they washed their garments they would remember. Wherever, whenever, or whatever—they would always remember the commandments of the Lord. They would always be wrapped up in His Word—the tallit (טלות, pronounced *tal-EET*).

Originally, the word *tallit* (also spelled *tallis*) meant "cloak," or "mantle"—a sort of blanket that men wore as they went about their daily lives in ancient times. At the four corners of this cloak, fringes were attached in accordance with the biblical commandment of Numbers 15:38–41.

After the Israelites were exiled from the land of Israel, as a result of being dispersed to different lands, they began to dress according to the fashion of the Gentiles around them. The tallit was no longer worn as a daily cloak; it became a religious garment—a prayer shawl—worn only at prayer time, at home, or in the synagogue. The synagogue is a building used for Jewish worship services, prayer, and study. It replaced the ancient temple or tabernacle of God's people.

The tallit is an authentic Jewish garment. Put simply, it is a rectangular-shaped garment with parallel stripes across the shorter ends. Most *tallitot* (plural of tallit) are white with navy or black stripes. It is important to note that it was originally woven without seams.

The tallit has fringes called *tzitzit* (זחזת) attached to each of its four corners, each having a cord of blue. It has a neckband called *atarah* (עטרה), which contains the Hebrew prayer recited before donning the garment. The garment can be made of only one of the following: linen, wool, silk, or synthetic material (polyester). The fabric of a tallit worn by a Levite should not be mixed.[2]

Wearing the tallit is a Jewish spiritual practice derived from a verse in the Torah, Numbers 15. The tallit is popularly known as a prayer shawl. In traditional

Judaism, the rabbis describe the Torah as "the garment of the soul," and the tallit is used to protect the scrolls of the Torah when they are moved. An old tallit that is unsightly, torn, or unusable gets donated to the synagogue or a Judaic library. It is then used to wrap worn out or superfluous documents, such as photocopies, that include the name *YHVH* (*Adonai),* the sacred name of God in Hebrew script, for burial with dignity in a *geniza,* a Jewish cemetery section set aside for this purpose.[3]

Even today the Jewish people say that the tallit is a religious symbol, a garment, a shroud, a canopy, a cloak that envelopes the Jew both physically and spiritually in prayer and celebration, and in joy and in sorrow.

The tallit is used at all major Jewish life events: circumcisions, *bar* and *bat mitzvahs,* weddings, and burials.

An interesting point to make at this juncture is that strictly observant Jewish men commonly wear a special four-cornered undergarment, called a *tallit katan* (טלות קטן, "little tallit"), so that they will have the opportunity to fulfill this important *mitzvah* (commandment) all day long. The tallit katan is worn under the shirt, with the tzitzit hanging out so they can be seen.

The *tallit gadol* (טלות גדול) is the large tallit worn

during prayers. It should be large enough to cover most of the wearer's body.

It is important to note that it is not the garment itself that makes the tallit special. The significance lies in the tzitzit, the fringes on the four corners. The purpose of the tallit, then, is to hold the tzitzit, and the purpose of the tzitzit according to the Torah is to remind us of God's commandments.

Chapter 2

What Are the Tzitzit?

*I*N ANCIENT TIMES, Hebrews were commanded to wear tassel fringes as a continuous visual reminder to strengthen the holiness in their lives by remembering and practicing God's (*YHVH*'s) commandments (Numbers 15:37–40; Deuteronomy 22:12).

Tassels were to be tied upon the four corners of the garment to remind the Israelites of the commandments of *YHVH*. This was to ensure a symbol of the commandments constantly before their eyes. Therefore, just by looking at the tallit with its tzitzit, the Jew was reminded of the commandments. It states in the Torah, "And when you see them, you shall remember all of God's commandments so as to keep them" (Numbers 16:39).

When referred to in the scriptures the word *fringe* is translated as "tassel," or "twisted thread." Therefore, the tassels were made of twisted white and blue thread and fastened upon each corner of the garment.

Another translation for the word *tzitzit* is "wings," but we will discuss this in more detail in a later chapter.

The blue color of the tzitzit was used to remind the Jews of the heavenly origin of the Law. It is interesting to note how the blue thread serves as a reminder.

Throughout the scriptures we can see, with study, that *YHVH* designed all of His creation to help reveal Himself to man. Jesus, God's Son *(Yeshua),* taught spiritual truths using common physical things around Him to help His disciples understand kingdom truths. Also, when the scriptures were written, *YHVH* ensured that the stories held truths of the physical realm. These stories, recounted in the Hebrew language, were all woven together to paint pictures that convey the spiritual truths that He designed for us to know. Usually these pictures are introduced at some point and then, through progressive revelation, we can see that they are built upon throughout the rest of the Holy Scriptures. These pictures can be unveiled with dedicated study, and this is an essential part of being able to "rightly divide the word of truth" (2 Tim. 2:15).

Therefore, to understand the significance of the blue color used in the tzitzit we need to remember that the fringes are a *YHVH*-given reminder to His people. The shade of blue used on the fringes is called *tekhelet* in Hebrew.[1] *Tekhelet* is also translated as the "color of the heavens." Hence, the *tekhelet* serves as a reminder that God's people are born from above and are called and required to reflect the nature of that heavenly kingdom while we live here on the earth.

The blue *tekhelet* thread originally had a purple hue of blue. It was obtained from extracting the gland of a specific snail. The only source was a small gland in the *Murex trunculus* snail. It took twelve thousand snails to fill up a thimble of blue dye.[2]

Blue is a color that is readily available today, so it is difficult to imagine that during the entire biblical period, blue was the most expensive color to produce. This is why it was only reserved for royalty. In 200 B.C., one pound of blue-dyed cloth cost the equivalent of \$36,000. By A.D. 300, this same pound of blue cloth cost \$96,000.[3] From this we can see that Lydia, the seller of purple and an early convert to Christianity, was one of the wealthiest women in the Empire.

> And a certain woman named Lydia, a seller of purple, of the city of Thyatira, which worshipped God, heard us: whose heart the Lord opened, that she attended unto the things which were spoken of Paul.
>
> —Acts 16:14

After some time, the secret of this blue dye was lost, and so generally, the custom has been to only use white fringes. Recently, a group of researchers in Israel have claimed that they can identify this specific snail *(Murex trunculus)*, and once again the blue dye is being manufactured.[4] However, it is important to note that not everybody accepts this as being the original tekhelet, but more and more people do put a blue thread among the fringes of their tallit.

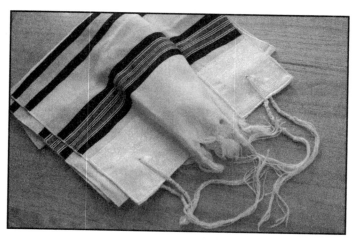

Tying tzitzit is a Jewish art, which could be described as a specialized form of macramé. Macramé is the ancient art of tying knots.[5] It is an alternative form of textile-making, using knotting rather than weaving or knitting. Its primary knots are the square knot and hitch knots. It has been used by sailors, especially in elaborate forms, to decorate the tools of their trade.

Four strands are inserted through the reinforced hole in each corner of the tallit: three short strands and one long blue strand. The longer strand is called the *shamash* and is used for winding around the others. When done correctly, the tzitzit will have a pattern of 7-8-11-13 winds between the double knots. There are five double knots in total.[6]

It is important to note that the 7-8-11-13 winding pattern is significant. There are several interpretations for this pattern of winding. One interpretation is that each set of windings corresponds to one of the four letters in God's name.[7] Seven and eight equals fifteen, which in *Gematria* (Jewish numerology) is equal to the two letters *yod* and *heh*, the first two letters of the name of God. Eleven is the equivalent of *vav* and *heh*, the last two letters of the name of God.

Thus they represent *YHVH*, the four-letter name of God. Thirteen is equivalent to the Hebrew word *echad (alef, chet, dalet)*, which means one. Hence, all four windings can be interpreted to say, "God is one." So to look at the tzitzit is to remember and know that "God is One."

In Gematria, the tzitzit (spelled *tzadi-yod-tzadi-yod-tav*) is equivalent to six hundred. To this we add the eight strands plus the five knots, totaling 613 in all. According to Jewish tradition, God gave 613 *mitzvot* (commandments) in the Torah. Just to look at them, therefore, is to remember all the mitzvot.

The central commandment surrounding tzitzit is:

> And you should see it and remember all of God's commandments and do them.
>
> —Numbers 15:39

Chapter 3

What Is the Atarah?

T HE TALLITOT USUALLY have an artistic motif of some kind along the top neck side. The motif or collar band is known as the *atarah* (crown). There is no particular religious significance to the atarah; it simply helps you to hold up the tallit the right way. However, it is common practice to write the words of the blessing for putting on the tallit on the atarah, so you can read the blessing while you are putting on the tallit.

It is important to note that the *tallit* is not blessed by rabbis (neither are any objects in the Jewish religion). Customarily, the person who uses the *tallit* says a blessing before he or she puts it on.

The following are examples of the blessing (*berachah*) which can be found embroidered on the atarah. We should stress at this point that these blessings are never generally said aloud unless a person is wearing his or her tallit.

Traditional Blessing

> *Blessed are You, Lord, our God, King of the universe, who has sanctified us with His commandments and commanded us to wrap ourselves in the tzitzit.*

Transliteration:

> *Baruch atah Adonai, Eloheinu, melekh ha'olam asher kiddeshanu bemitsvotav vetsivanu lehitattef batsitsit.[1]*

Messianic Blessing

> *Blessed are you, O Lord, King of the universe, who has fulfilled all of the law through Yeshua the Messiah and have covered us with His righteousness.*

Transliteration:

Baruch atah Adonai, Eloheinu, melekh ha'olam asher milla et kol hatorah biyashu hamashiach ikissa et kulanu vetsedkato.[2]

It is important to note that if a blessing is written on your tallit, you should not bring the tallit into the bathroom with you. Sacred writings should not be brought into the bathroom. In the Jewish community many synagogues have a tallit rack outside the bathroom. There will usually be a sign that tells you to remove your tallit before entering.

Chapter 4

Wearing a Tallit

A TALLIT IS USUALLY worn by a Jew who has reached the "age of majority" (commandment age). The age of majority is similar to "coming of age" or "age of maturity" in other cultures. In most Jewish communities, this would be the age of thirteen for a boy (*bar mitzvah*) and age twelve for a girl (*bat mitzvah*). (These terms refer to both the individual reaching this age and to the ceremony that often accompanies this milestone.)[1] This is the age when a young person is recognized as an adult.

It is important to note that traditionally the tallit was worn only by men, but with the development of non-orthodox movements (conservative and reform), more and more women are wearing a tallit for prayer.

It is a traditional practice that the tallit is worn only during the morning prayers, with the exception of the *Kol Nidre* service during Yom Kippur.[2]

Yom Kippur is the Sabbath of Sabbaths and is observed on the tenth day of the Hebrew month of *Tishri*, which corresponds to September or early October in the secular calendar. It is the Jewish holiday of the Day of Atonement referenced in Exodus 30:10, Leviticus 16:29–30, Leviticus 23:27–31, Leviticus 25:9, and Numbers 29:7–11.

> And the LORD spake unto Moses, saying, Also on the tenth day of this seventh month there shall be a day of atonement: it shall be an holy convocation unto you; and ye shall afflict your souls, and offer an offering made by fire unto the LORD. And ye shall do no work in that same day: *for it is a day of atonement*, to make an atonement for you before the LORD your God.
> —Leviticus 23:26–28, emphasis added

The day is commemorated with a twenty-five-hour fast (specified as twenty-five hours and not twenty-four to ensure that the fast commences before the Sabbath begins). Individuals are supposed to refrain from eating and drinking even water and participate in intensive prayer. It is considered the holiest day of the Jewish year. It is also important to note that Yom Kippur is a complete Sabbath, so all work is forbidden on this day. The fast begins before sunset on the evening before Yom Kippur and ends after nightfall on the day of Yom Kippur.

It is a day set aside to "afflict the soul," to atone for the sins of the past year. Simply put, Yom Kippur is the day to ask forgiveness for promises broken to God. It should be noted that the day before is reserved for asking forgiveness for broken promises between people.

In addition to the restrictions already mentioned, the following are also refrained from during Yom Kippur—anointing with perfumes or lotions, marital relations, bathing, and wearing leather shoes.

The evening service that begins Yom Kippur is commonly known as *Kol Nidre,* meaning "all vows." It is during this first service that the tallit is worn.

According to Jewish tradition, the act of putting on the tallit only has "religious merit" if it is done during daylight. Therefore, it is not normally worn at a Friday evening service, or any other evening service.

It became customary to put on a tallit for Kol Nidre since it was still daylight at the time the service commenced. The tallit was then left on throughout the entire evening of the Yom Kippur service.

Therefore, although it is traditional that the tallit is only worn for morning prayers (during daylight), the exception of Kol Nidre is accepted along with two other occasions, one of which is the evening service of *Simchat Torah* ("Rejoicing in the Torah"). This holiday marks the completion of the annual cycle of weekly Torah readings with special Friday evening services that include a Torah reading as the Torah scrolls are then removed from the ark of the covenant.[3]

In biblical times the Jewish men wore the prayer shawl all the time, not just at prayer. In New Testament times, ordinary people only wore a tallit on special occasions, if at all. It was the Pharisees who seem to have worn it regularly and, apparently in some cases, often for show. Jesus does not express disapproval of the custom itself, but He does condemn the extra-long fringes that the Pharisees wore to display their piety, declaring them hypocrites and therefore a bad example.

> And when thou prayest, thou shalt not be as the hypocrites are: *for they love to pray standing in the synagogues and in the corners of the streets, that they may be seen of men.* Verily I say unto you, They have their reward. But thou, when thou prayest, enter into thy closet, and when thou hast shut thy door, pray to thy Father which is in secret; and thy Father which seeth in secret shall reward thee openly.
>
> —Matthew 6:5–6, emphasis added

Then spake Jesus to the multitude, and to his
disciples, Saying, The scribes and the Pharisees
sit in Moses' seat: All therefore whatsoever they
bid you observe, that observe and do; but do not
ye after their works: for they say, and do not.
For they bind heavy burdens and grievous to
be borne, and lay them on men's shoulders; but
they themselves will not move them with one of
their fingers. But all their works they do for to
be seen of men: they make broad their phylacteries, *and enlarge the borders of their garments.*
                      —Matthew 23:1–5, emphasis added

Everything they do is done for show. They act
holy by wearing on their arms little prayer boxes
with Scripture verses inside, *and by lengthening
the memorial fringes of their robes.*
                      —Matthew 23:5, TLB, emphasis added

The words *phylacteries* or *tefillin* do not appear in
the Old Testament. *Phylacteries* appears only once in
the New Testament. The word *phylacteries* is translated from the Greek word *phulakterion,* meaning a
guard case or a leather pouch,[4] used in the instances
above for wearing scrolls of the Torah passages.

Taking into consideration these scriptures, we
should ensure that the tallit is worn with the right
motives of the heart to obtain the full spiritual benefit
of this sacred tradition.

Wearing a tallit is still relevant today when you consider what we have learned so far. When you wrap yourself in the prayer shawl during prayer you create your own personal space around yourself. The reason why it is good to create this private space is to isolate yourself from the environment and to keep you focused. By doing this you symbolically strengthen your commitment to your time of prayer.

Wearing the tallit is quite straightforward. Open or unfold your tallit and hold it in both hands so you can see the atarah. Recite the blessing. After reciting the blessing, throw the tallit over your shoulders like a cape and bring your hands together in front of your face briefly, covering your head for a moment of private meditation. Then adjust the tallit comfortably on your shoulders.

If the prayer shawl has the traditional blessing on the atarah, it is customary to kiss the ends of the neckband where the last word and the first word of the blessing are written.

If you are thinking of wearing a tallit there are several scriptures on which you can mediate. The following verses in Psalm 104 are very popular and spoken often:

> Bless Adonai, O my soul. Adonai, My God,
> You are very great, You are clothed in glory

and majesty. You have wrapped yourself with a garment of light, spreading out the heavens like a curtain.

—Psalm 104:1–2

Bless the LORD, O my soul. O LORD my God, thou art very great; thou art clothed with honour and majesty. Who coverest thyself with light as with a garment: who stretchest out the heavens like a curtain: Who layeth the beams of his chambers in the waters: who maketh the clouds his chariot: who walketh upon the wings of the wind...O LORD, how manifold are thy works! in wisdom hast thou made them all: the earth is full of thy riches...The glory of the LORD shall endure for ever: the LORD shall rejoice in his works. He looketh on the earth, and it trembleth: he toucheth the hills, and they smoke. I will sing unto the LORD as long as I live: I will sing praise to my God while I have my being. My meditation of him shall be sweet: I will be glad in the LORD. Let the sinners be consumed out of the earth, and let the wicked be no more. Bless thou the LORD, O my soul. Praise ye the LORD.

—Psalm 104:1–3, 24, 31–35

Chapter 5

The Tallit: The Covering

*I*N Middle Eastern culture it is traditional for the
man to cast a garment over the one being claimed
for marriage. This was clearly demonstrated in the
book of Ruth when Ruth lay at the feet of Boaz.

> And it came to pass at midnight, that the man was
> afraid, and turned himself: and, behold, a woman
> lay at his feet. And he said, Who art thou? *And
> she answered, I am Ruth thine handmaid: spread
> therefore thy skirt over thine handmaid* [make me
> your wife]; for thou art a near kinsman.
> —Ruth 3:8–9, emphasis added

The tallit is often used as a covering. The bride and
bridegroom are covered with the tallit during a Jewish
wedding ceremony (traditionally called *Kiddushin*).[1] It
forms a canopy under which the whole wedding party
stand. The wedding ceremony is performed under the
tallit. The tallit is held up during the ceremony by

four poles called *chuppah* or *huppah*. One custom is to have honored friends hold the chuppah poles. In some families, the custom is to make a family chuppah and to pass it down from generation to generation (as opposed to a wedding dress). The chuppah represents the home that they will create together and the Divine Presence under which they will be married.

During the final benediction the couple is wrapped in two tallitot that are placed around their shoulders. In some communities, the bride and groom are wrapped together by a single tallit. In others the bridegroom covers his bride with his tallit, signifying that he is taking her into his care.

The groom will continue to use the tallit in his married life and would hope to present it to a future son upon his *bar mitzvah*. Also, often the children born to the couple will be wrapped in the same tallit when they are named.

There is also a custom that the bride presents the groom with a tallit on the day of the wedding. This is because the tallit also represents the number thirty-two, which is the number of fringes on the shawl. The number thirty-two is the numerical equivalent of the Hebrew word for *heart*.[2]

Chapter 6

The Tallit: The Mantle

AS WE HAVE previously mentioned, the tallit is also known as a cloak, robe, coat, or mantle. We know that it was a commandment of God that the four corners of the garment have the tzitzit attached so that God's people would be constantly reminded to obey His Law. When we take note of these facts we can then begin to see various places in the scriptures where the tallit is mentioned and the implications or relevance of the events that occur.

For example, in 1 Samuel 15:26–28 we read about Samuel the prophet informing Saul that he is no longer King of Israel.

> And Samuel said unto Saul, I will not return with thee: for thou hast rejected the word of the LORD, and the LORD hath rejected thee from being king over Israel. And as Samuel turned about to go away, *he laid hold upon the skirt of*

his mantle, and it rent. And Samuel said unto him, The LORD hath rent the kingdom of Israel from thee this day, and hath given it to a neighbour of thine, that is better than thou.

—1 Samuel 15:26–28, emphasis added

It is clearly not a coincidence that in Saul's distress he grabbed hold of Samuel's mantle, or more specifically, the skirt of the mantle (representing God's Law), which is translated "wing," the *tzitzit.* He grabbed so tightly that Samuel's mantle tore. Samuel makes it clear that because Saul rejected the Word of the Lord or commandment of God, he had been rejected as king. Furthermore, just as he tore the mantle, the kingship would be torn from him.

There is also the suggestion in scripture that the mantle is transferred or passed on to a successor, son, designated relative, or servant.

And it shall come to pass, that him that escapeth the sword of Hazael shall Jehu slay: and him that escapeth from the sword of Jehu shall Elisha slay. Yet I have left me seven thousand in Israel, all the knees which have not bowed unto Baal, and every mouth which hath not kissed him. *So he departed thence, and found Elisha* the son of Shaphat, who was plowing with twelve yoke of oxen before him, and he with

the twelfth: *and Elijah passed by him, and cast
his mantle upon him.*

—1 Kings 19:17–19, emphasis added

In 1 Kings 19 God speaks to Elijah and makes it
clear that his successor is to be Elisha, so Elijah goes
and finds Elisha and casts his mantle on him. Elisha
recognizes the call of God on his life and leaves
everything to follow Elijah. When Elijah's ministry
is over, the anointing that comes to rest on Elisha
is that of Elijah and of Elijah's mantle (2 Kings 2:8,
13–15). Many believe that Elijah's mantle was
symbolic of the power of prayer that Elijah had satu-
rated it with.

> And *Elijah took his mantle*, and wrapped it
> together, and smote the waters, and they were
> divided hither and thither, so that they two went
> over on dry ground. *He [Elisha] took up also
> the mantle of Elijah that fell from him*, and went
> back, and stood by the bank of Jordan; *And he
> took the mantle of Elijah that fell from him, and
> smote the waters*, and said, Where is the LORD
> God of Elijah? and when he also had smitten
> the waters, they parted hither and thither: and
> Elisha went over. And when the sons of the
> prophets which were to view at Jericho saw
> him, they said, *The spirit of Elijah doth rest on*

> *Elisha.* And they came to meet him, and bowed
> themselves to the ground before him.
> —2 Kings 2:8, 13–15, emphasis added

The words of Zechariah in the scripture that follows are particularly profound, demonstrating that all nations will embrace and reverence the Word of the Lord or the commandment of God, which is depicted by the holding of the skirt mentioned in Zechariah 8. The majority of Jewish points of reference (such as rabbinical sources, sages throughout the ages, and Jewish writing and commentary) stress the fact that the commandments or Law were given to the Jews. Because of this, the tallit and, more significantly, the tzitzit are considered in many circles not to be relevant to the Gentile (non-Jew).[1] However, I believe that this passage of scripture demonstrates to us that Christians all over the world, of all nations and tongues, will be drawn to the ancient language of God and therefore ancient truths which have been generally overlooked.

> And the inhabitants of one city shall go to another, saying, Let us go speedily to pray before the LORD, and to seek the LORD of hosts: I will go also. Yea, many people and strong nations shall come to seek the LORD of hosts in Jerusalem, and to pray before the LORD. Thus

saith the LORD of hosts; In those days it shall
come to pass, that ten men shall take hold out
of all languages of the nations, *even shall take
hold of the skirt of him that is a Jew,* saying, We
will go with you: for we have heard that God is
with you.

—Zechariah 8:21–23, emphasis added

It is not by coincidence that so may non-Jews have
begun a journey of discovery that literally brings the
Scriptures to life.

In the Jewish community a type of mantle is also
used to cover and store the Torah when it is not being
read. The Torah is handwritten in Hebrew, the oldest
Jewish language. It is also called the Law of Moses
(*Torat Moshe*). The Torah primarily refers to the first
five books of the Hebrew Bible: Genesis, Exodus,
Leviticus, Numbers, and Deuteronomy. The Torah is
also known as the Five Books of Moses or the *Penta-
teuch* (Greek for "five containers," which refers to
the scroll cases in which the books were being kept).
For Jews, the Torah was traditionally accepted as the
literal word of God as told to Moses. A portion of it
is read each week in the synagogue. It takes a year to
complete the readings.[2]

The Torah mantle is usually made from luxu-
rious fabrics with intricate embroidery that is usually

symbolic of key events in Jewish history, demonstrating the unique style of Jewish art.

The Torah mantle's sole use is to cover and protect the Torah it contains. Traditionally the Torah is kept in a curtained-off area known as the ark of Law. The rabbi lifts the Torah and its mantle out of this space in front of the congregation.

Creation began with God's command: "Let there be light," signifying the beginning of the divine light of God in the world (Genesis 1:3). It seems logical that the Torah is often described in imagery as light. For example, *Torah Orah* means "the Teaching of Light."[3]

One might ask the question, why mention the Torah mantle at all, as it becomes clear from study that it is completely different from the tallit. The relevance is simple. The main purpose of the tallit is to hold the tzitzit. The main purpose of the tzitzit is to remind us of the commandments of Yahweh. It seems apt therefore to ensure that we understand what the commandments of Yahweh are or at least know where we can find them, as the Torah contains the Law of God.

Chapter 7

The Tallit: Little Tent

THE WORD *TALLIT* is often translated as "little tent." This is, however, incorrect, as *tal* means "dew"[1] and the Hebrew word for "little" is *qatan*.[2] Therefore a literal interpretation of *tallit* as "little tent" is inappropriate. Nonetheless, from an etymological viewpoint we can still accept this phrase. In Mishnaic Hebrew the word *tallit* means "to cover," from the Hebrew *tillel* ("to cover"); from the Aramaic *tallel*, also meaning "to cover;" and from the word *telal*, meaning "shade," which has Semitic roots.[3] Taking the uniqueness of this language into consideration, we can see that over the centuries the practice of wearing the tallit has become widely accepted in most Jewish circles as symbolic of the wearer being enclosed in his own little tent. The Tent of Meeting or Tabernacle, as it was also known, could not accommodate over six million Jews at any one time. Therefore, the tallit served them as their own private sanctuary where they could meet with God.

Each man had his own prayer shawl, or tallit. Each man would pull his tallit over his head, forming a tent, where he would begin to chant and sing Hebrew songs and call upon God. It was intimate, it was private and set apart from anyone else, enabling the men to totally focus upon God. Their tallitot were their prayer closets!

It is often said that when Balaam blessed Israel he looked out from the mountain and saw God's people resting in their tents and in their tallitot and was moved to speak prophetically.

> And when Balaam saw that it pleased the LORD to bless Israel, he went not, as at other times, to seek for enchantments, but he set his face toward the wilderness. And Balaam lifted up his eyes, *and he saw Israel abiding in his tents* according to their tribes; and the spirit of God came upon him. And he took up his parable, and said, Balaam the son of Beor hath said, and the man whose eyes are open hath said: He hath said, which heard the words of God, which saw the vision of the Almighty, falling into a trance, but having his eyes open: *How goodly are thy tents, O Jacob, and thy tabernacles, O Israel!*
> —Numbers 24:1–5, emphasis added

Scholars also comment on the occupation of the apostle Paul *(Sha'ul)*, who was a Jewish Pharisee and also a tentmaker. As the tzitzit are usually tied under the supervision of a rabbi, many believe that he made tallitot, tents for prayer and not tents to live in.[4]

So we see that as the atarah (collar) was placed over the head, it formed a little tent—a little tabernacle. As the individual meditated, prayed, and chanted, often the hands would be held up and out. This gave the tallit the appearance of having wings. The "wings of the tallit" are discussed in the next chapter.

Chapter 8

The Tallit: The Wings

*T*HE FOUR CORNERS of a tallit with its fringes are also called the wings of the tallit. As the Atarah is placed over the head, it forms the wearer's own tent. The wings of the garment are formed when the arms of the wearer are held out.

In Numbers 15:38, the word *border* or *corner* is translated from the Old Testament Hebrew word in *kanaf*, which can also mean "wings." For this reason, the corners of the prayer shawl are often called wings. The Hebrew word *kanaf* occurs in Psalm 91 where God's people are encouraged to "abide under the shadow of the Almighty" and also to trust in the protection given "under His wings."

> He that dwelleth in the secret place of the most High shall abide under the shadow of the Almighty. I will say of the LORD, He is my refuge and my fortress: my God; in him will

I trust. Surely he shall deliver thee from the snare of the fowler, and from the noisome pestilence. He shall cover thee with his feathers, *and under his wings (kanaf) shalt thou trust*: his truth shall be thy shield and buckler.

—Psalm 91:1–4, emphasis added

In Ezekiel 16:4–8 the word *skirt* can also be translated "wing," which is the same Hebrew word used in Numbers 15. In Ezekiel 16, the Lord speaks to His people in an imagery passage saying:

And as for thy nativity, in the day thou wast born thy navel was not cut, neither wast thou washed in water to supple thee; thou wast not salted at all, nor swaddled at all. None eye pitied thee, to do any of these unto thee, to have compassion upon thee; but thou wast cast out in the open field, to the lothing of thy person, in the day that thou wast born. And when I passed by thee, and saw thee polluted in thine own blood, I said unto thee when thou wast in thy blood, Live; yea, I said unto thee when thou wast in thy blood, Live. I have caused thee to multiply as the bud of the field, and thou hast increased and waxen great, and thou art come to excellent ornaments: thy breasts are fashioned, and thine hair is grown, whereas thou wast naked and bare. Now when I passed by thee, and looked upon thee, behold, thy time was the time of love; *and I spread my skirt [kanaf] over thee, and covered thy naked-ness:* yea, I sware unto thee, and entered into a covenant with thee, saith the Lord GOD, and thou becamest mine.

—Ezekiel 16:4–8, emphasis added

When we consider the interpretation of the skirt as wings, the significance of this passage of scripture becomes clear. The Lord is speaking to His people recounting that at the time they became a nation they were loathed and hated by all the heathen nations surrounding them. They were immature and polluted by their own sins, but He spoke a Word to His people, declaring that they should live. Once that Word was spoken, the passage shows how God's people increased in number, wealth, and glory. We can see that, despite the condition of His people, God did not forsake them but looked on them in love. Using the translation of the word *skirt* to *wings,* we can begin to understand that when God speaks about spreading His skirt over His people it can be interpreted as the Lord spreading His tallit over His people. The Lord makes it clear in this passage that His people have reached a place where they are ready for love and for commitment.

Therefore, He spreads His tallit over them in the same way that a husband might spread his tallit over his bride during a Jewish wedding ceremony. The Lord makes it clear that He is ready to make a promise to His people and to enter into covenant with them so that they truly become His people and He becomes their God. The act of entering into a covenant could then be seen to be represented by His skirt, or wings—His tallit with the tzitzit—His commandments being accepted by His people as a statute forever.

Another phenomenon linked to the wings of the tallit is divine healing. As we look at key passages of scripture we find a significant link between the tallit and miraculous accounts of healing in the New Testament.

In various New Testament scriptures we can see where this translation of the fringes as wings becomes relevant. This translation is important when we consider the meaning of the word used for "border" or "hem" in the New Testament: the Greek word *kraspedon,* which is also translated "fringe" or "tassel."[1]

> And whithersoever he entered, into villages, or cities, or country, they laid the sick in the streets, and besought him that they might touch if it were but *the border of his garment*: and as many as touched him were made whole.
>
> —Mark 6:56, emphasis added

> And when the men of that place had knowledge of him, they sent out into all that country round about, and brought unto him all that were diseased; And besought him that they might *only touch the hem of his garment*: and as many as touched were made perfectly whole.
>
> —Matthew 14:35–36, emphasis added

In these accounts we find occasions where people were healed as they touched the hem or border (significantly the wings or fringes) of Jesus' garment. It is generally understood that Jesus, as an orthodox Jew, wore a tallit. Therefore, it is widely taught that it wasn't specifically the hem or border of the garment that people were reaching for but the tzitzit. The story of the healing of one particular woman in the New Testament is told in three of the Gospels (Matthew 9:20–22; Mark 5:25–34; Luke 8:43–48), giving us an insight into several aspects of healing connected to the tzitzit, the wings.

> And, behold, a woman, which was diseased with an issue of blood twelve years, came behind him, *and touched the hem of his garment*: For she said within herself, If I may but touch his garment, I shall be whole. But Jesus turned him about, and when he saw her, he said, Daughter, be of good comfort; thy faith hath made thee

whole. And the woman was made whole from
that hour.

—Matthew 9:20–22, emphasis added

And a woman having an issue of blood twelve
years, which had spent all her living upon
physicians, neither could be healed of any,
Came behind him, *and touched the border of
his garment:* and immediately her issue of blood
stanched. And Jesus said, Who touched me?
When all denied, Peter and they that were with
him said, Master, the multitude throng thee and
press thee, and sayest thou, Who touched me?
And Jesus said, Somebody hath touched me: for
I perceive that virtue is gone out of me. And
when the woman saw that she was not hid, she
came trembling, and falling down before him,
she declared unto him before all the people for
what cause she had touched him and how she
was healed immediately. And he said unto her,
Daughter, be of good comfort: thy faith hath
made thee whole; go in peace.

—Luke 8:43–48, emphasis added

Why would this woman stoop to touch the tzitzit,
the wings of Jesus' garment? Why not His hands, or
His feet? It was clear that she had heard about Jesus
and about the miracles that had happened. Perhaps
she realized that she didn't need to touch Him or need

Him to touch her but that she just needed to touch His wings in faith, believing to be healed. Perhaps the Old Testament passage in Malachi became a reality to her in that moment. Before her very eyes, not far from her trembling grasp, stood the manifested embodiment of those ancient words.

> But unto you that fear my name shall *the Sun of righteousness arise with healing in his wings;* and ye shall go forth, and grow up as calves of the stall.
> —Malachi 4:2, emphasis added

Just a few feet away from her faltering steps stood the Son of Righteousness, and she believed with all her heart that He had *healing in His wings* for her that day.

Chapter 9

The Tallit: The Word

*I*N THE PREVIOUS chapter we looked at the account of the woman with the issue of blood. She had suffered from this abnormal condition of bleeding for twelve years. The story of her healing is significant for yet another reason. When we look closer at the accounts relating to her healing (Matthew 9:18–25; Mark 5:22–43; Luke 8:43–56), we realize that there was a dialogue already in progress and that Jesus was on His way to heal someone else when she received her healing from Him. Jesus had been approached prior to her arrival by Jairus, a ruler of the synagogue, requesting that He come and heal his daughter.

> While he spake these things unto them, behold, there came a certain ruler, and worshipped him, saying, My daughter is even now dead: but come and lay thy hand upon her, and she shall live. And Jesus arose, and followed him, and so did his disciples. And, behold, a woman, which was diseased

with an issue of blood twelve years, came behind him, and touched the hem of his garment:

—Matthew 9:18–20

And, behold, there cometh one of the rulers of the synagogue, Jairus by name; and when he saw him, he fell at his feet, And besought him greatly, saying, My little daughter lieth at the point of death: I pray thee, come and lay thy hands on her, that she may be healed; and she shall live. And Jesus went with him; and much people followed him, and thronged him. And a certain woman, which had an issue of blood twelve years, And had suffered many things of many physicians, and had spent all that she had, and was nothing bettered, but rather grew worse, When she had heard of Jesus, came in the press behind, and touched his garment.

—Mark 5:22–27

And, behold, there came a man named Jairus, and he was a ruler of the synagogue: and he fell down at Jesus' feet, and besought him that he would come into his house: For he had one only daughter, about twelve years of age, and she lay a dying. *But as he went the people thronged him.* And a woman having an issue of blood twelve years, which had spent all her living upon physicians, neither could be healed of any, Came behind him, and touched the

border of his garment: and immediately her
issue of blood stanched.

—Luke 8:41–44, emphasis added

It is important to realize that the Bible is not a
book of coincidences or accidents. Every word is
divinely inspired by God. Therefore, it is generally
accepted that throughout the Bible details are given
which purposefully aim to guide the reader to a
specific point. One thing in particular which drew
my attention was the fact that the woman with the
issue of blood had suffered for *twelve years* and also
that Jairus's daughter was also *twelve years old* (Mark
5:42; Luke 8:42). This suggested to me that these two
events were divinely linked for some reason and that
there was definitely more to this story.

After the woman is healed Jesus continues on His
journey with Jairus but is interrupted by a servant
from Jairus's house informing him that there is no
need for Jesus to come; his daughter had died.

While he yet spake, there came from the ruler
of the synagogue's house certain which said,
*Thy daughter is dead: why troublest thou the
Master any further?* As soon as Jesus heard the
word that was spoken, he saith unto the ruler
of the synagogue, Be not afraid, only believe.

—Mark 5:35–36, emphasis added

Jesus admonishes him not to fear but to believe, and they continue on their journey to the house. On arrival at the house Jesus makes a point of removing all the mourners and the general family members from the room, allowing only Peter, James, John, and her mother and father to enter.

At this point we see where the healing of the woman with the issue of blood becomes significant. The key is connected to the action of touching. To understand the significance of the touching that is taking place we need to first understand a particular aspect of Jewish Law. According to the Law, one could become ritually unclean simply by touching or coming into contact with someone or something that was unclean. The Law specified that a woman experiencing bleeding was considered unclean, and the dead were considered unclean.

> And if a woman have an issue of her blood many days out of the time of her separation, or if it run beyond the time of her separation; all the days of the issue of her uncleanness shall be as the days of her separation: she shall be unclean.
>
> —Leviticus 15:25

> He that toucheth the dead body of any man shall be unclean seven days.
>
> —Numbers 19:11

Therefore, from the perspective of the Law the woman should not have been among the crowds surrounding Jesus, as everyone who came into contact with her would also be considered unclean. From the text we can see that when she is questioned by Jesus she is clearly embarrassed and ashamed as she declares that she has indeed broken the Law.

> But the woman fearing and trembling, knowing what was done in her, came and fell down before him, and told him all the truth. And he said unto her, Daughter, thy faith hath made thee whole; go in peace, and be whole of thy plague.
>
> —Mark 5:25–34

> And when the woman saw that she was not hid, she came trembling, and falling down before him, she declared unto him before all the people for what cause she had touched him and how she was healed immediately.
>
> —Luke 8:47

When this woman touched the hem of Jesus' garment, He would have been deemed unclean in the eyes of the Law. This is important to note, as Jesus later enters the room of the dead girl (also considered unclean) and takes hold of her hand. (A rabbi would not normally do this, as such an action would render Him unclean.) This issue of cleanliness and uncleanliness was no longer an issue by the time He reached Jairus's home, as Jesus had already come into contact with the woman with the issue of blood.

Here we see how a series of events flow together to bring Jesus to the room of a twelve-year-old dead girl. The accounts in the Gospels of Mark and Luke seem to agree that the young girl lay dying. Jesus is on His way to heal her. He is interrupted by the woman with issue of blood. The delay results in time passing in which the little girl dies, so Jesus is no longer expected to heal her but to raise her from the dead. Surely people would marvel more over a girl raised from the dead than one healed from sickness. One might consider that God had divinely ordered the events to bring Him the greater glory.

> But when he had put them all out, he taketh the father and the mother of the damsel, and them that were with him, and entereth in where the damsel was lying. *And he took the damsel by the hand, and said unto her, Talitha, cumi;* which is, being interpreted, Damsel, I say unto thee, arise. And straightway the damsel arose, and walked; for she was of the age of twelve years. And they were astonished with a great astonishment. *And he charged them straitly that*

no man should know it; and commanded that
something should be given her to eat.
     —Mark 5:40–43, emphasis added

Inside that room a miraculous event takes place
which centers around two words, "Talitha, cumi,"
and the touch of the hand of Jesus. *Talitha cumi* is
Aramaic and is generally interpreted as "damsel
arise" or "daughter, I say unto thee, arise."[1] However,
several experts in this field tend to agree that there is
more meant by these two little words than has been
initially interpreted. One could also concur that as
we know she was twelve years old and under Jewish
law considered a woman, the emphasis in translation
would not be "little girl."

Scholars have suggested that if Jesus had said and
meant, "Young girl, arise," He would have used the
Aramaic word *talya* and the possibly absolute form,
talyatha, not *talitha*. The Aramaic absolute form of
tallit is *tallitha*. Further investigation also suggests
that if Jesus had meant to say "damsel arise," He
would have said *Talyatha, qumi*, not *Talitha, cumi*.[2]

A key fact which helps us to arrive at a conclusion
is found in what was the usual Jewish practice in the
circumstances of death. It is customary for a Jewish
male to be buried in his tallit. It is also customary for

a female corpse to be covered with a tallit while being prepared for burial.

We begin to see a deeper meaning for the words Jesus uttered on that day. It is probable that this young woman was lying on her deathbed covered in a tallit or wrapped in a tallit as a burial shroud, symbolizing the fact that their daughter was under the hand of the Almighty and subject to His tender mercies. Her father, being a synagogue official, understood the significance of the tallit and the tzitzit. He knew the promises of God are to bring health and healing to those who adhered to His commandments and devoted their life to Him. It should also be noted that in translation *talitha* is also connected to the words for "lamb" and also for "covering."[3] When we take into consideration the fact that the word *talitha* is also connected to "covering," we arrive at a more revelatory understanding of the words *Talitha, cumi:* Young woman (who is covered by the tallit), arise.[4] Such a statement would surely have been marvelled at by the girl's parents and warranted Jesus' stipulation of secrecy, especially as the New Testament scriptures record only three canonical instances where Jesus raised the dead.[5] In making that statement and affirming it with the miracle, He had declared His deity (He was God in the flesh) to all present—a fact

He did not want to become public knowledge, as His time had not yet come.

We can further look at the spiritual significance of this miracle when we consider that the girl was wrapped in a tallit with tzitzit (representing the commandments of God or the Word of God) and that Jesus is the Lamb of God, the Word become flesh.

> In the beginning was the Word [Jesus], and the Word was with God, and the Word was God.
> —John 1:1

> *And the Word was made flesh*, and dwelt among us, (and we beheld his glory, the glory as of the only begotten of the Father,) full of grace and truth.
> —John 1:14, emphasis added

The scene that thus presents itself is unique: Jesus, the manifested Word of God, raises the daughter of Jairus, who is wrapped up in the Word. This is a truth that we as believers should grasp hold of—when God is presented with His Word He can do nothing else but fulfill it and be moved by it.

Chapter 10

A Final Note

W ITH THE GROWING popularity of the tallit among Christians, it is generally said that Christians should not or are not obliged to wear a tallit or embrace its spiritual truths, as the laws regarding it were only given to the Jewish nation and not to the Gentiles. Whereas it is true that Christians are not obliged to adhere to many of the laws prevalent in the Jewish way of life, the merits of many Jewish customs become significant when considering the events portrayed in the Bible in their original context. Therefore, it is not surprising that Christians are drawn to many of these practices, as they have their roots in the Bible, the Holy Word of God.

Taking on board the promises of the New Testament, Christians everywhere can enjoy and benefit from this sacred rite.

For all who are led by the Spirit of God are sons of God. And so we should not be like cringing, fearful slaves, but we should behave like God's very own children, adopted into the bosom of his family, and calling to him, "Father, Father [Abba, Abba]."

—Romans 8:14–15, TLB

So God's blessings are given to us by faith, as a free gift; we are certain to get them whether or not we follow Jewish customs if we have faith like Abraham's, for Abraham is the father of us all when it comes to these matters of faith.

—Romans 4:16, TLB

Abraham had the same experience—God declared him fit for heaven only because he believed God's promises. You can see from this that the real children of Abraham are all the men of faith who truly trust in God. What's more, the Scriptures looked forward to this time when God would save the Gentiles also, through their faith. God told Abraham about this long ago when he said, "I will bless those in every nation who trust in me as you do." And so it is: all who trust in Christ share the same blessing Abraham received.

—Galatians 3:6–8, TLB

But Christ has bought us out from under the doom of that impossible system by taking the curse for our wrongdoing upon himself. For it is written in the Scripture, "Anyone who is hanged on a tree is cursed" [as Jesus was hung upon a wooden cross]. Now God can bless the Gentiles, too, with this same blessing he promised to Abraham; and all of us as Christians can have the promised Holy Spirit through this faith.

—Galatians 3:13–14, TLB

Christians everywhere are enjoying special times of prayer using their tallitot. It is so awesome that so much symbolism could be encompassed in one piece of cloth. The tallit serves as an eternal reminder of God's commandments, His constant love for His people, His promises, His divine protection, and His healing power.

Each time that you pray in your tallit may you recall that this action is symbolic of you being wrapped up in God's Word. I pray that the divine presence of the Holy Spirit will be more real to you each time you pray in your own "little tent," and each time that you look at the tzitzit may you remember God's Word and to obey it. Remember that the God that you serve has healing in His wings.

Endnotes

Chapter 1—What Is a Tallit?

1. "A List of the 613 Mitzvot," Judaism 101, http://www.jewfaq.org/613.htm (accessed October 5, 2007).

2. Adam Barnett, "The Tales of the Tallit," Articlesbase.com, http://www.articlesbase.com/religion-articles/the-tales-of-the-tallit-70679.html (accessed October 5, 2007).

3. Shraga Simmons, "Geniza," Ask Rabbi Simmons on About.com, http://judaism.about.com/library/3_askrabbi_o/bl_simmons_geniza.htm (accessed October 5, 2007).

Chapter 2—What Are the Tzitzit?

1. *Strong's Exhaustive Concordance*, s.v. "tekelet (8504)" (Grand Rapids, MI: Associated Publishers and Authors, Inc.).

2. Levi bar Ido, "Why the Hassle Over Tassels?" http://www.bnaiavraham.net/newpage/tassels.pdf (accessed October 5, 2007).

3. Ibid.

4. Mois A. Navon, "Historical Review of Tekhelet and the Hillazon," *P'til Tekhelet*, The Association for the Promotion and Distribution of Tekhelet. http://www.tekhelet.com/timeline.htm (accessed October 5, 2007).

5. "Macramé," Target Woman, http://www.target woman.com/articles/macrame.html (accessed October 8, 2007).

6. "Tallit Talk," Rabbi Scheinerman's Home Page, http://www.scheinerman.net/judaism/tallit/ (accessed October 5, 2007).

7. Ibid.

Chapter 3—What Is the Atarah?

1. Arba Kanfot, "Wearing the Tallit Katan," Hebrew for Christians, http://www.hebrew4christians.com/ Blessings/Daily_Blessings/Tallit_Katan/tallit_katan .html (accessed October 5, 2007).

2. The Three Arches Company, Ltd., HolyLandShopping.com, s.v. "The New Covenant Prayer Shawl." http://holylandshopping.com/ product_info.php?cpath=23_62&products_id=38 (accessed October 5, 2007).

Chapter 4—Wearing a Tallit

1. "Bar Mitzvah, Bat Mitzvah, and Confirmation," Judaism 101, http://www.jewfaq.org/barmitz.htm (accessed October 8, 2007).

2. "Kol Nidrei," http://www.iyyun.com/holidays/ YomKippur/Kol%20Nidrei.html.

3. "Simchat Torah," Hebrew for Christians, http:// www.hebrew4christians.com/Holidays/Fall_ Holidays/Simchat_Torah/simchat_torah.html (accessed October 5, 2007).

4. *Strong's Exhaustive Concordance*, s.v. "phylactery (5440)" (Grand Rapids, MI: Associated Publishers and Authors, Inc.).

Chapter 5—The Tallit: The Covering

1. Mordechai Becher, "The Jewish Wedding Ceremony," OHR.edu., http://ohr.edu/yhiy/article .php/1087 (accessed October 5, 2007).

2. "What Happens During a Jewish Wedding?" Usenet FAQ, http://www.faqs.org/faqs/judaism/FAQ/04- Observance/section-65.html (accessed October 8, 2007).

Chapter 6—The Tallit: The Mantle

1. YahChannah Wolf, "Do Not Study Torah, Gentile!" Qumran Bet Community, http://www.qumran.com/ do_not_study_torah_gentile.htm (accessed October 8, 2007).

2. "Torah Readings," Judaism 101, http://www.jewfaq .org/readings.htm (accessed October 8, 2007).

3. "Torah Mantles," Harwin Studios, http://www .harwinstudios.com/commissions/torah.php (accessed October 8, 2007).

Chapter 7—The Tallit: Little Tent

1. *Strong's Exhaustive Concordance*, s.v. "tal (2919)" (Grand Rapids, MI: Associated Publishers and Authors, Inc.).

2. *Strong's Exhaustive Concordance*, s.v. "ith (6996)" (Grand Rapids, MI: Associated Publishers and Authors, Inc.).

3. *TheFreeDictionary.com*, s.v. "tallis." http://www .thefreedictionary.com/tallis (accessed October 8, 2007).

4. "Little Tent, a Prayer Closet." Highland Shepherd Resources, http://www.msgr.ca/msgr-8/Prayer_ Shawls_2.htm (accessed October 8, 2007).

Chapter 8—The Tallit: The Wings

1. *Strong's Exhaustive Concordance*, s.v. "kraspedon (2899)" (Grand Rapids, MI: Associated Publishers and Authors, Inc.).

Chapter 9—The Tallit: The Word

1. John D. Garr, "The Hem of His Garment," The Restoration Foundation. http://www.restoration foundation.org/goldenkey/hem_13.htm (accessed October 8, 2007).

2. Ibid.

3. *Strong's Exhaustive Concordance*, s.v. "talitha (5008)," "taleh (2924)," and "tela (2922)" (Grand Rapids, MI: Associated Publishers and Authors, Inc.).

4. Gary Collet and Debra Collet, "Talit—The Jewish Prayer Shawl," Jews 4 Jesus. http://www.jews4jesus .co.uk/scripture/talit_shawl.html (accessed October 8, 2007).

5. "Miracles of Jesus," AboutBibleProphesy.com, http://www.aboutbibleprophecy.com/miracles.htm (accessed October 8, 2007).